50 Years

Of

Season's Greetings

Nothing in Common

Printed in the United States of America

ISBN 979-8-9861868-1-8

Happy

Holidays!

Introduction

It's been fifty years...

September 15, 1973 - September 15, 2023

I, Joseph, take you, Karen,
to be my wife. I promise
to be true to you, in good times
and in bad, in sickness
and in health. I will love you
and honor you all the days of my life.

I, Karen, take you, Joseph,
to be my husband. I promise
to be true to you, in good times
and in bad, in sickness
and in health. I will love you
and honor you all the days of my life.

A few of our family and friends have been with us for all of our fifty years together. Others have joined us somewhere along the way. But however long you've known us, we thought this holiday season we'd invite you to look back on our fifty years together, to relive old memories with us, if you have them, or to peek into our earlier years together, if you don't, and to make of those years what you will.

For us, these fifty years have passed quickly. They say time flies when you're having fun, and it must be true: we've spent these years getting to know more about what love really means, and we've always had fun sending our best wishes to the people we love the most. So, once again, we wish you peace, joy and happiness in 2024 and in all the years to come, and with this book, we hope you'll see how much our family and friends have *always* meant to us.

Karen Joe

We were married in September of 1973. When Joe's grandfather passed away six months later, we decided to continue his practice of drawing his own Christmas cards, which he'd been doing since 1928. We wanted to use the cards to chronicle the growth of our family, as he had done his. The expected birth of our first child, due in December, 1974, seemed a perfect way to begin.

 1974

Kate was born December 15th, and our own family was off to a promising start.

Of course, the new baby in the house made it hard to get a good night's sleep.

 1975

WAA-
AAH!
WISHING YOU PEACE THROUGHOUT
THE COMING YEAR... KAREN, JOE AND
OUR PRECIOUS KATHRYN ELIZABETH -
LOVE - US

1976 1977

With Joe working days and attending law school at night, 1976 and 1977 found him too busy to draw Christmas cards, especially after Jennifer was born. But a law school class titled "the Philosophy of American Constitutionalism" interested him in the American experiment in government. A quick quotation from Thomas Jefferson was easier than trying to draw an accurate likeness of the new baby girl or her older sister.

> A wise and frugal government, which shall restrain men from injuring one another, which shall leave them otherwise free to regulate their own pursuits of industry and improvement, and shall not take from the mouth of labor the bread it has earned. This is the sum of good government.
>
> — Thomas Jefferson

Pretty lame. (We know.) More than a few friends remarked on the lack of holiday spirit. (We hoped for better things once law school was over.)

After graduation, Joe got a job in Tampa. We put our Miami home up for sale and spent the last few months of 1978 living out of our suitcases at the in-laws' house in Clearwater.

Drawing good likenesses was never Joe's strength. So when he managed a reasonable likeness of Kate in 1979, he chose not to try his luck a second time.

After Daniel joined the family in 1980, Joe attempted to draw all three children, while Kate – not yet six – contributed the actual lettering.

Finally, halfway decent likenesses of Jen and Dan!
But when the card made Kate look chubby (she was not), Joe was scolded soundly.

Shaken by the experience, he looked for ways to avoid drawing likenesses.

Translation:

"The clumsy Christmas artist has started to cheat with the camera."

 1983

Everyone agreed that the camera was more accurate than Dad's pen, but now Kate and Jen were old enough to give him a hard time about having to pose for photographs.

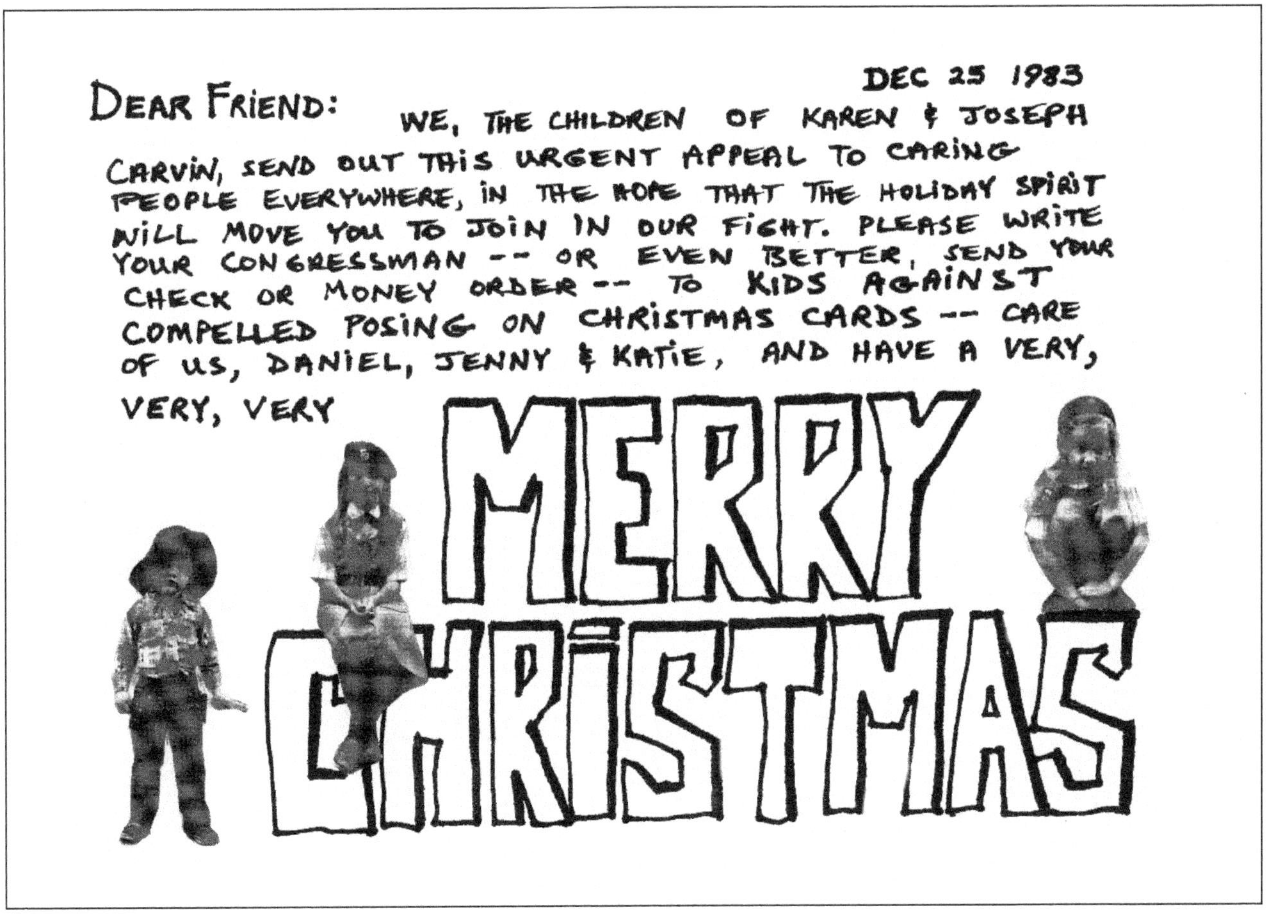

Tessa, our fourth, was yet another big baby. (They'd ranged from over nine pounds to over twelve, and Karen had given birth to all of them naturally!) She obviously deserved recognition for the feat - but in Joe's imaginary world, credit went to the Stork.

So. What's with the new outfit? MARKETING! That's right. Your STORK has finally wised up. That other fellow's got not a THING that I don't have... but he gets all the attention! Case in point: KATIE CARVIN. 9 LBS 14 OZ at birth. She's in LOVE with the FAT GUY because he brought her a measly 2 LB doll one year. (And he only carried it one night, too.) JENNY CARVIN was 9 LBS 4 OZ. Does she sing "The STORK is Coming to Town"? And DANIEL CARVIN: 12 LBS. 7 OZ! I've had back trouble ever since, and he doesn't even know me....

WELL, NO MORE. TESSA CARVIN (10 LBS 9 OZ) hasn't been brain-washed yet with all that "Ho-Ho-Ho!" and I've still got time. So - how do I look?

Listen, I've got to run. Got a TV commercial to do! (It was my chiropractor's idea.) So this year, please, THINK STORK! CELEBRATE THE GIFT OF LIFE!

HAPPY BIRTHDAY TO EVERYBODY FROM KAREN AND JOE CARVIN & FAMILY. 1984.

The family was growing, but we found that coming up with new ideas for cards was harder than expected.

 1985

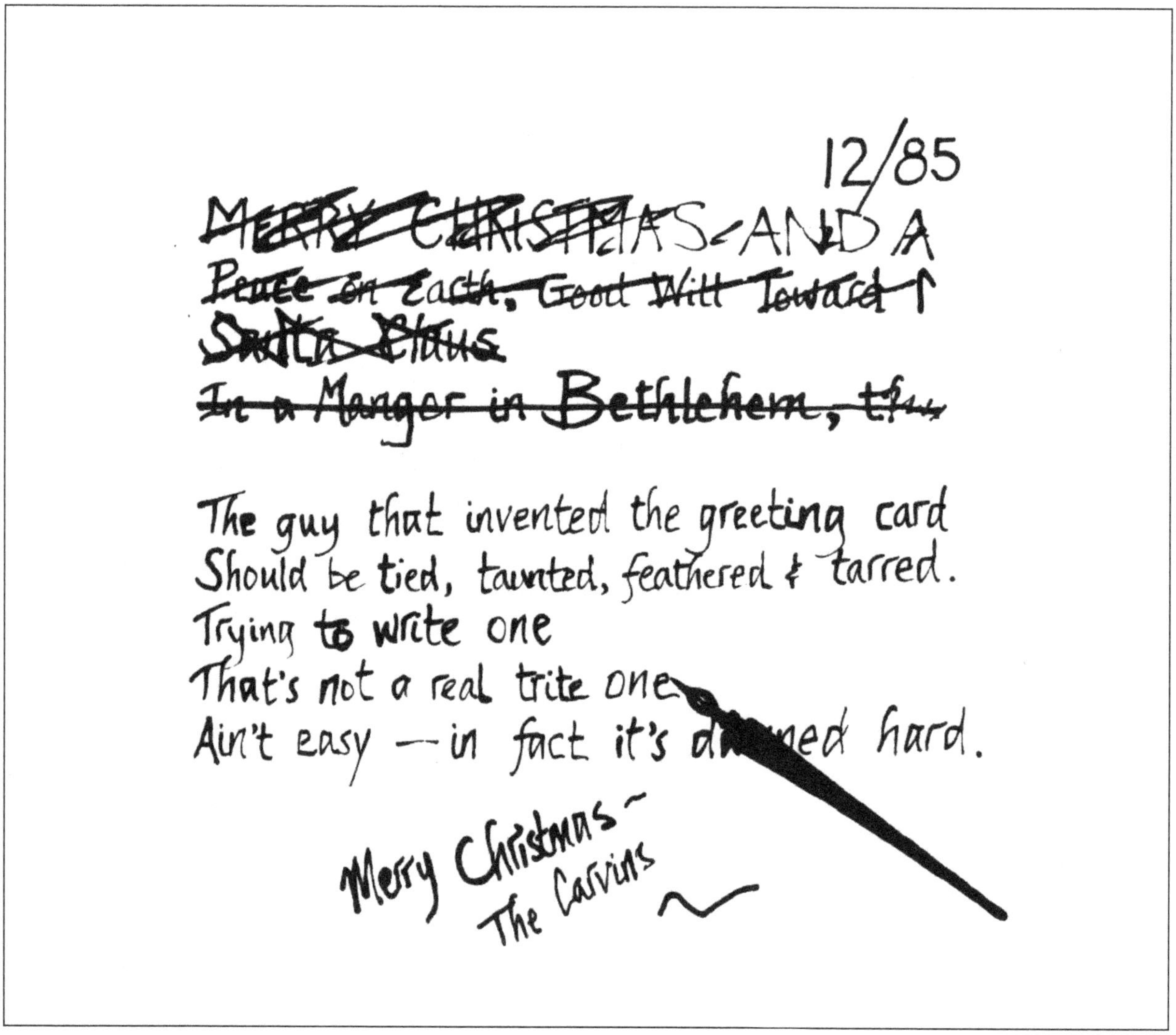

12/85

~~MERRY CHRISTMAS AND A~~
~~Peace on Earth, Good Will Toward~~
~~Santa Claus~~
~~In a Manger in Bethlehem, the~~

The guy that invented the greeting card
Should be tied, taunted, feathered & tarred.
Trying to write one
That's not a real trite one
Ain't easy — in fact it's damned hard.

Merry Christmas ~
The Carvins

 1986

Our church friends had started wondering aloud why our cards didn't have anything to do with "the reason for the season." So we attempted to satisfy them.

Sort of.

 1986

THE JOY OF THE YULETIDE SEASON CAN BE REDUCED TO A SINGLE WORD – ENTHUSIASM!
WORD ORIGINS BY ERIC PARTRIDGE

'ENTHUSIASM' – the noun comes from Greek 'ἐνθουσιασμος,' 'divine inspiration'

from ἐν (in) + θεος (god).

Wishing you Enthusiasm of the BEST kind this season –

KAREN – JOE – KATIE – JENNY – DANIEL – TESSA

THE CARVINS

12/25/86

Fast as our family was growing, technology was growing even faster. Our new Tandy 1000SX computer inspired the 1987 card.

THE CARVIN TIMES

Lutz, Florida "All the News that Fits" December 25, 1987

CARVINS GET NEW COMPUTER, OPT FOR NEW STYLE CHRISTMAS CARD – FRIENDS SHOCKED

Lutz, Fla. Modern technology has arrived at the Carvin house. *Times* correspondent Bob Wordword has learned that the Carvins are planning this year to make their Christmas card using their new Tandy 1000SX computer. In an exclusive *Times* interview, Karen and Joe Carvin refused to confirm or deny the report, but did admit that using a computer was a lot easier than trying to draw a card. Friends of the family, who report hearing assorted beeps, buzzers and keyboard noises from the Carvin house until the wee hours of the morning, are uniformly dismayed by the news. "It's been a tradition," says family neighbor and long-time Lutz resident Homer Fornswitch, lamenting the loss of the old Carvin pen-and-ink drawings. "These computers are taking over the world. Next thing you know, we'll be putting a man on the moon." Friends of the family who prefer the more traditional approach to Christmas cards are meeting next Monday night at 7 p.m., at the Fornswitch home on Old Lutz Dirt Trail Road, in downtown Lutz. Homer is planning "one of them protest marches." Sadie Fornswitch will be serving up lemonade and hard cider to one and all.

Tessa Carvin, 3, expresses the view of many of the Carvins' friends.

DANIEL CARVIN BREAKS INTO SOCCER STARDOM!

Forest Hills, Fla. Daniel Carvin has shed the white robe and orange belt of Tae Kwan Do, and has donned the green jersey and shin guards of the Forest Hills Blue Falcons Soccer Club, where he and some other 7 year olds have a winning record.

Says Dan, pulling off his shoes and soiled green socks, "Now, I can truly say I've experienced the thrill of victory, and the agony of de feet."

CARVIN SISTERS APPROACH LIFE WITH MIXED EMOTIONS: SOMETIMES ENTHUSIASM, MORE OFTEN MORTIFICATION

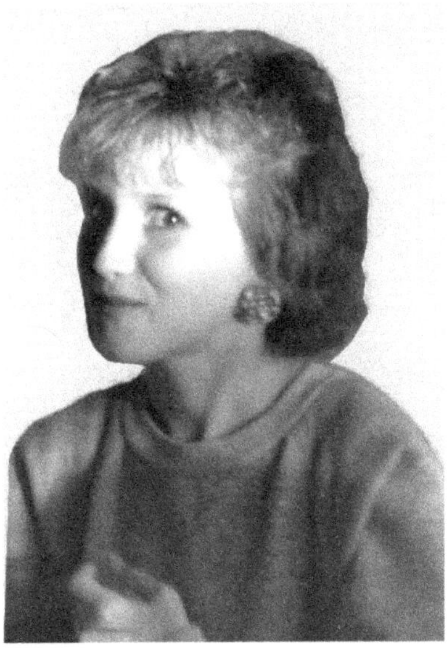

Upstairs. Kati Carvin, who was featured in the very first Christmas card ever published by the Carvin Times Publishing Company back in 1974, has come a long way since that first appearance. As long-time subscribers may recall, she was then so shy she wouldn't come out to pose for the artist, and had to be drawn still inside the "oven."

At 13, Kati is often bright and enthusiastic – as when cheering on the Scream Team for the Buchanan Bucs. Around home, she can usually be located on the floor of her room, amid assorted clothes strewn all over. Kati dreams of someday having her own telephone up there. Maybe if Santa got her one, our *Times* reporter Bob Wordword could tap the line and find out what's going on up there behind that cool exterior.

Nye Park. This reporter, asking around Lutz for Jenny Carvin, quickly learned that she rarely leaves Nye Park – home of the Lutz Leaguerettes softball club. When not slugging away from the batter's box, Jenny can be found there as one of the Nye Park "Tigers" cheerleaders, rapping away in support of one of the Nye Park boys' flag football teams.

Asked for an interview, Jenny was not at a loss for words: "Yeah, yeah, yeah; gonna do it, gonna do it, gonna yeah yeah do it…"

Jenny is not always so articulate. Asked if she'd mind her picture being taken for this issue of the *Times*, Jenny could only roll her eyes and shrug her shoulders. (We're told it can be mortifying to be 10.)

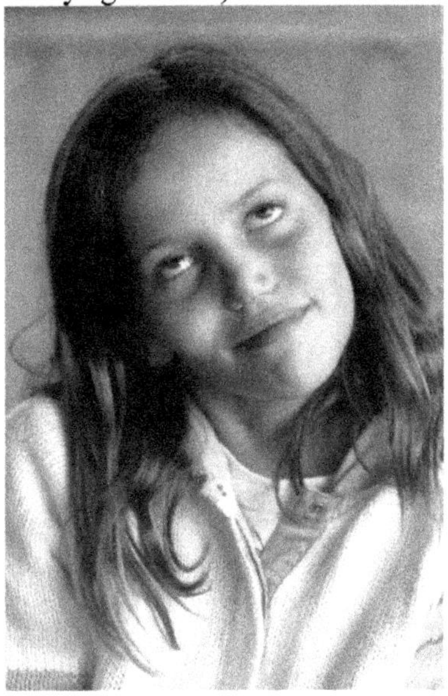

 1988

AFTER FOURTEEN YEARS OF CHRISTMAS CARD IDEAS, THE OLD GUY HAS FINALLY HAD IT. THE FAMILY DECIDES THAT ITS TIME TO TRADE HIM IN FOR A NEW MODEL.
CAUTION HAZARDOUS WASTE

STOP
ALL HE NEEDS IS A LITTLE FUEL
$19.88
CHRISTMAS CHEER !!!!
HOPE YOUR HOLIDAY IS A GAS
The Carvins
HOW ABOUT A LITTLE HOLIDAY SPIRITS?
JWC

THIS CHRISTMAS
WE THOUGHT
WE MIGHT
PLAY A LITTLE

 1989

 1990

The front and inside of the 1990 card was blank white card stock.

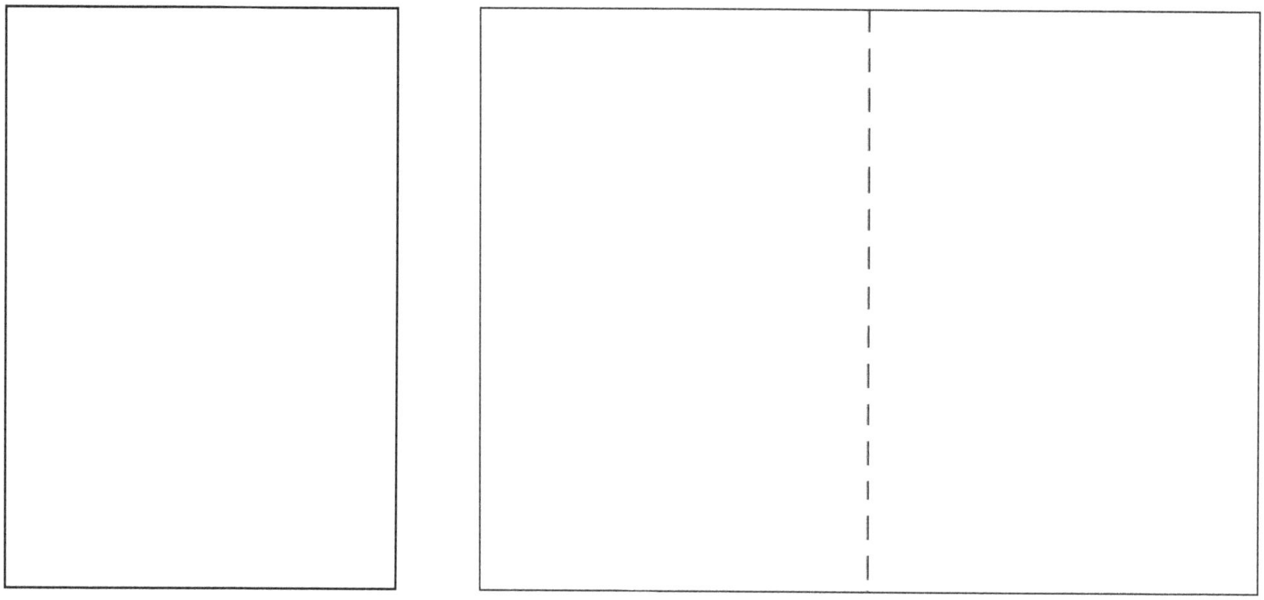

Inserted between the blank pages was a poem written in the style of Poe's "The Raven." But in our version, the writer was not haunted by memories of a lost Lenore, he was a do-it-yourself holiday card drawer haunted by writer's block and the nagging temptation to do what normal people do: go to the store and buying a ready-made Hallmark card.

12-25-90

We'll Do Our Own Card, Evermore

Once, upon a midnight dreary, while I pondered, weak and weary,
Over many a quaint and curious idea for a Christmas card,
While I nodded, nearly napping, suddenly there came a tapping,
As of something gently rapping, rapping in my pencil drawer.
"Tis some rat or roach," I muttered, "Scratching in my pencil drawer –
Only this, and nothing more."

Ah, distinctly I remember, it was in the bleak December,
Sheets of crumpled drawing paper lay discarded on the floor.
Hard I'd pressed for inspiration; long I'd fought off strong temptations
To give up on my card creations, buy the darn things at the store –
Buy some mass production pictures sold to others by the score –
But I'd insisted: nevermore.

And the silken, sad, uncertain rustling of each purple curtain
Thrilled me – filled me with fantastic terrors never felt before;
So that now, to still the beating of my heart, I stood repeating,
"Tis some rat or cockroach eating something in my pencil drawer –
Some small rat or cockroach eating sweets the kids left in the drawer –
This it is, and nothing more."

 1990

My ideas had all been dreadful; I'd been getting quite a headful
Of perverted thoughts that people whom we mail to would deplore.
So I looked at cards from past years, concentrated hard on last year's,
Fought back all those hard and fast fears that this card would be a bore,
That this year's card would be forgotten as a witless yuletide bore,
Guaranteed to make friends snore.

Late into the wee hours dreaming, long I sat there, thinking, scheming,
Hoping for some thought I'd never plagiarized before;
But my writer's block unbroken, inspiration gave no token,
Till I thought I heard there spoken two unseemly words: "The store."
Close I listened, and again I heard the muffled words, "The store!" –
Merely this, and nothing more.

Back to pad and pen then turning, all my soul within me burning,
Soon again I heard a scratching, somewhat louder than before.
"Surely," said I, barely mumbling, "It's a cockroach, merely rumbling
In my papers, likely fumbling for some food, or to explore –
Let my heart be still a moment and this mystery explore; --
Tis a roach and nothing more."

Thereupon, I lit a candle, found a heavy, wooden sandal,
Thinking I could safely handle any rat, I pulled the drawer:
Therein sat, I found (by golly) a picture-perfect Santa, jolly,
Sitting in a wreath of holly, on a Hallmark from the store,
Sat there on a store-bought Hallmark, midst the cards we'd got before –
Sat and watched me, nothing more.

Then this tiny elf beguiling my sad fancy into smiling
By the custom-tailored styling of the red suit that he wore,
"Though thy beard be white and thick, sir, you can't really be Saint Nick, you're
Just some stationery picture from the mall that I abhor –
State your proper business, mister; tell me what you're looking for."
Quoth the Santa, then, "The store."

Much I marveled at this midget, how he got there, how he did it,
Though his answer little meaning, little relevancy bore;
For you cannot help agreeing that no living human being
Ever yet was blest with seeing Santa in a pencil drawer,
Sitting in a wreath of holly, on a Hallmark in a drawer,
Saying just those words: "The store."

But this Santa, sitting lonely in the cluttered drawer, spoke only
Those two words, as if his soul in those two words he did outpour.
Nothing further then he uttered – neither stammered then, nor stuttered –
Til I scarcely more than muttered, "Oh well, others have drawn cards before;
On the morrow, it will hit me, as ideas have come before."
Then he said, again, "The store."

Startled at the stillness broken by these words so clearly spoken,
I thought, doubtless, since he talks, he must be able to say more;
Perhaps some crafty merchandiser, thinking me a tightwad miser,
Sent this sneaky advertiser, thinking I could not ignore
A messenger subliminal, so smugly sitting in my drawer,
Whispering through the night, "The store."

I knew I had no brilliant vision, knew I needed a decision,
Some small spark to get it going, something worth this struggling for,
So to all inspiring saints, who bring good things to those who cain't,
I made a fervent wish, a plaint: "Please, help me draw one Christmas more!
Some new pen and ink creation, something witty, I implore!"
But this Santa said, "The store."

Then methought the words grew louder, amplified by some keen power
Beating in my brain to force me to the car, then to the store.
"Wretch," I cried, "Hallmark hath sent thee! You've been hired to torment me!
We won't spend a single cent! We'll *draw* our cards here, as before!
If we have to leave it blank, we'll do our own again!" I swore.
But Santa grinned, and said, "The store."

"Be these words our sign of parting, saint or fiend," I shrieked, upstarting.
"Get thee back to Macy's, or some mall department store!"
And with that I grabbed the sandal, held it in my upraised hand, till
Up he jumped and out he ran, till far he fell from out the drawer,
Till hard he fell, and landed, bruised, and fearful, ran across the floor…
(We'll do our own card, evermore.)
– The Carvins

Lest the Hallmark Santa's fate be unclear, the back side of the otherwise-blank folding card depicted his fate.

But as the next year proved, Hallmark Santa had a lot of friends. And when writer's block returned a year later, they would not go away.

The names of the books on the shelves in the '91 card:

"Guide to the Best Colleges."
"Guide to the Cheapest Colleges."
"Winning Softball."
"No More Cats!"
"Nintendo Power."
"Kayak."
"The Great Whitewater Rivers of Lutz."
"The Night Before Christmas."
"How to Draw."
"The Ghost of Christmas Past."
"The Raven," by Edgar Allen Poe.
"How to Cope with Writer's Block."

And most importantly,

"Revenge of the Hallmark Santas."

Karen had taken up quilting, and because of Joe's new job, we moved to a new house, in a new neighborhood.

CHRISTMAS FUTURE...
(WE HOPE TO BE MOVING BY APRIL 1993)
9314 WELLINGTON PARK CIRCLE
TAMPA, FLORIDA 33647
I-275
I-75
S.R. 581
HUNTER'S GREEN
B. DOWNS
BRUCE
Exit 56
N
BEARSS AVE
I-4
S.R. 581
HUNTER'S GREEN DRIVE
HUNTER'S GREEN
WELLINGTON PARK CIRCLE
"STONE BRIDGE"
KAREN, JOE, KATHRYN, JENNY, DANIEL AND TESSA CARVIN

The 1993 card was a tribute to grandfather Carvin. Our cover was taken from his 1954 Card, which had invited recipients to "look in on" his family.

"YES... YOU DON'T SAY.... YES.... YES.... YES..... YES.... RIGHT...... NO, I DON'T THINK JOE'S DONE THE CARD YET. PUT RELIGION IN IT THIS YEAR? YOU'VE GOT TO BE KIDDING! WE'LL BE LUCKY IF IT'S SOMETHING WE CAN EVEN SEND TO OUR FRIENDS FROM CHURCH"
~MOM~
"JUST AS LONG AS YOU DON'T MAKE ME LOOK FAT, DAD, I REALLY DON'T CARE WHAT YOU DO..."
~JEN~ 16
"HEY FOLKS! I THOUGHT I'D SURPRISE YOU AND COME HOME FOR THE WEEKEND!
~KATE~ 19
LAUNDRY
F.S.U
AND MAYBE DO A LITTLE LAUNDRY WHILE I'M HOME..."
SO... 1993 HAS BEEN GOOD...
... LET'S MAKE 1994 EVEN BETTER OK?
"GIVE ME A SENSE OF HUMOR, LORD, GIVE ME THE GRACE TO SEE A JOKE TO GET SOME HAPPINESS FROM LIFE AND PASS IT ON TO OTHER FOLK"
—FROM HIS 1954 CARD
MERRY CHRISTMAS
MEANWHILE, DOWN AT THE CLINTON CLINIC:
"HEALTH PLAN, PLEASE, HILARY..."
"BUT DOC— HOW COME BORIS ONLY NEEDS A GOOD DOSE OF FREE ENTERPRISE?"
~TESSA~ 9
"WHATEVER YOU DO, DO NOT ASK ME ABOUT THAT POEM I WROTE. YOU KNOW — THE ONE ABOUT LOVE..."
~ME~
"THE MOST LOGICAL THING TO GET ME FOR CHRISTMAS WOULD NOT NECESSARILY BE MORE BOOKS--AFTER ALL, I'LL BE ABLE TO GET MOST OF THE BOOKS I'LL NEED FROM THE LIBRARY. BESIDES, I'M PROBABLY TOO CEREBRAL ALREADY — NOW, A PAIR OF HOCKEY GOALIE GLOVES WOULD REALLY ROUND OUT MY PERSONALITY...."
~DAN~ 13
"THIS CARD IS DONE IN THE STYLE OF MY GRANDFATHER, CHARLEY CARVIN, WHO STARTED DRAWING HIS OWN CHRISTMAS CARDS IN 1928. AS HE WOULD HAVE SAID — HAVE A HAPPY NEW YEAR —"
"From the CARVINS"

c:\win\winword\seasons greetings\ "Merry Christmas 1994 from Karen, Joe, Kate, Jennifer, Dan and Tess Carvin." Now let's see if we can figure out how to get this thing to print.......#$!@#! ..... #$!@#! ....(yawn...) .....#$!@#!......(yawn) ...SNZSN... szzzsznz

SEASONS GREETINGS
From the Carvins
Kathryn:
Hi. Merry Christmas! You know, I'm graduating this year, and I think I've finally decided what I want to do with my life. Seeing that people are so messed up and need so much help and all, I think I'll go into Public Health. Either that or -- maybe I'll be a birthing coach. Well actually, either one of those two things or an archaeologist...
Jennifer:
Look, Dad. I go to college, I work at Publix, I babysit, and I 'll soon start a second job at USF. I have a car payment to make, not to mention auto insurance, and repairs. I work all the time and still I never have any money ...
So I just don't need you giving me a hard time right now, okay? If you want to poke fun at me, let people know I'm nearly nineteen but I'm not sure I'm ready to leave home...
Karen:
No Joe, I don't think Santa Claus in jail shackled with a ball and chain exactly captures the spirit of Christmas-- I don't care how you tie it in.
MY opinion? If you want to say something about politics, put it in an insert we can send just to your friends. I really think we want this to be a Christmas card, dear. You know : reindeer or something. Please?
Daniel and Tessa, Enjoying the holiday too much to comment for the card:
You know, when you think about it, Karen's right. I'll leave the politics for some other time. A Christmas card should be warm and
send friendly thoughts to the people you love. It should not make fun of anyone in the family and should certainly not remind people of the uglier sides of life, such as the fighting
that goes on in some families. A Christmas card should be colorful, with reds and greens and white snow and Bing Crosby, and it should be hand drawn on good, textured paper, or done with watercolors that feature extinct or endangered species like the Audubon Society puts out, or --
Hey, wait a minute... That would mean I'd have to start all over again from scratch! HECK NO!
IF YOU WANT THAT, YOU'LL HAVE TO WAIT UNTIL NEXT YEAR ! MEANWHILE, HAVE A GOOD HOLIDAY.
©1995

 1996

WARNING:
WE'RE GOING TO MAKE YOU
WORK THIS YEAR . . .

Do you know who we are?

You've probably already guessed,
we're the Carvins. (Karen & Joe & Family)
Who else would send you such a *brash* card?

But do you *REALLY* know us?

Now you can brush up on your knowledge of our family -- simply complete the **Carvin Family Trivia Quiz.**
When you do,

the initial letters of your answers will
spell out a message from us!

(Read that last sentence again -- it is VERY IMPORTANT)

Furthermore, you can transfer each letter, by number, to the **Puzzle Square** on the third page, and receive a second, **BONUS MESSAGE!**

We've even started the first message for you!

Good Luck ! . . . . (P.S. It's easy if you follow the instructions)

12-25-96

 1996

CARVIN FAMILY TRIVIA QUIZ

ANSWERS

a. Our Scottish Greatgrandfather gave his small Texas Ranch this name	a.	W _ _ (115 5 140)
b. Chore the young man of the house does faithfully	b.	E _ _ _ _ _ _ _ _ _ _ _ _ (142 41 72 46 35 153 145 12 49 146 68 40 194)
c. Jennifer works hard to maximize her minimum ________.	c.	_ _ _ _ _ (54 176 187 139 135)
d. A liqueur named for the Carvin family dog (or for Mrs. O'Leary's cow?)	d.	_ _ _ _ _ _ _ _ _ _ (77 4 16 148 80 144 14 175 59 11)
e. What Dad's monkey did from the tree limbs in '62	e.	_ _ _ _ _ (78 157 183 17 91)
f. The household projects Dad still hasn't gotten to?	f.	_ _ _ _ _ _ _ _ _ (116 161 74 119 167 58 37 61 164)
g. Wind-up string toy from Mom's youth	g.	_ _ _ _ (43 169 15 2)
h. North Carolina River where Dad's kayak longs to play	h.	_ _ _ _ _ (123 20 29 21 102)
i. What the family that prays together achieves	i.	_ _ _ _ _ (132 156 120 141 98)
j. What "X" (see below) strives to be at the courts	j.	_ _ _ _ _ _ _ _ _ _ (155 179 134 18 122 32 87 89 110 95)
k. Kate and Braden's big day	k.	_ _ _ _ _ _ _ _ (101 62 90 70 178 117 13 88)
l. One of Dad's many uses for that ol' demon rum....	l.	_ _ _ _ _ _ (26 34 63 190 99 1)
m. "_____ ____ virgin mother & child..."	m.	_ _ _ _ _ _ _ _ (103 186 162 22 38 8 160 57)
n. Second of the notes Dad croons at karaoke	n.	_ _ (133 172)
o. Word that goes well with "truly" and "sincerely"	o.	_ _ _ _ _ (168 109 100 104 185)
p. Jennifer's middle name	p.	_ _ _ _ _ _ _ (127 9 143 51 107 191 189)
q. Where we play golf and tennis	q.	_ _ _ _ _ _ _ _ _ _ _ _ _ _ _ _ _ _ _ _ _ _ _ (154 56 60 23 158 163 96 53 81 64 111 47 124 48 174 33 177 69 181 79 25 170 171)
r. Though over 9 pounds, Jen was still the ____ of the litter. ("X" was 12 lbs. 7 oz.)	r.	_ _ _ _ (94 10 126 75)
s. What Mom is, when not painting	s.	_ _ _ _ _ _ _ _ _ _ (82 130 30 73 173 71 39 44 149 83)
t. What Uncle Chris may do if you don't play your cards right	t.	_ _ _ _ _ _ _ _ _ _ _ _ (152 66 182 19 27 7 50 67 85 55 180 108)
u. Now 12, she was named "4th" (in Greek)	u.	_ _ _ _ _ (159 45 6 137 86)
v. Chore the young man of the house hates to do	v.	_ _ _ _ _ _ _ _ _ _ (165 92 138 97 76 129 105 166 184 131)
w. What Mom uses for that special, "crafty" touch	w.	_ _ _ _ _ _ _ _ _ _ _ (136 65 84 147 193 113 24 31 42 112 188)
x. What Mom and Dad have (& Johnny Cash doesn't?)	x.	_ _ _ _ _ _ _ _ _ _ _ _ _ _ _ (114 36 121 28 192 150 125 93 3 151 52 106 128 118)

Puzzle Square - & Bonus Message

	1L	2g	3x		4d	5a	6u	7t		8m	9p	10r		11d	12b	13k
14d	15g		16d	17e	18j	19t	20h	21h	22m	23q	24w		25q	26L	27t	
28x	29h	30s	31w	32j	33q	34L		35b	36x	37f		38m	39s	40b	41b	42w
43g		44s	45u	46b		47q	48q	49b	50t	51p	52x	53q		54c	55t	56q
57m	58f		59d	60q		61f	62k	63L	64q	65w		66t	67t	68b	69q	70k
	71s	72b	73s	74f		75r	76v	77d	78e		79q	80d	81q	82s	83s	84w
85t	86u	87j		88k	89j	90k		91e	92v	93x		94r	95j	96q	97v	
98i	99L	100o		101k	102h	103m	104o	105v		106x	107p	108t	109o	110j	111q	112w
113w	114x		115a	116f	117k	118x	119f		120i	121x	122j	123h	124q	125x	126r	127p
128x		129v	130s	131v	132i	133n	134j	135c		136w		137u	138v	139c	140a	141i
142b	143p		144d	145b	146b	147w	148d	149s	150x	151x	152t		153b	154q	155j	156i
	157e	158q		159u	160m		161f	162m	163q	164f		165v	166v	167f		168o
169g	170q		171q	172n	173s	174q	175d	176c	177q	178k		179j	180t		181q	182t
183e	184v	185o				186m	187c	188w	189p	190L		191p	192x	193w	194b	

[For answers, see final pages of this book]

Hi! Dan here. Employed at Chick-Fil-A and looking forward to going to college. The folks wanted me to point out that Dad only agreed to draw this year's card on the condition that Mom agree to paint it. But what I really want to talk about is my new car. It's a really zippy, bright red Nissan 2000, with a removable "T-" top...
What's new with Jen? Not much. I'm working at the Museum of Science & Industry, mostly. Oh, I guess I did go "spelunking" in October— that was cool! Way under ground! And in September, I jumped out of an airplane from 13,000 feet up. That was awesome! (I have a great video of my free fall.) There was my trip to Thailand in July. And to Bali. And to Jakarta...
This is Tessa. Have you forgotten what it's like to be 13? In case you have: I do not have a job. I do not have a car. I didn't go spelunking, or sky-diving, or on a trip to Jakarta. What have I been up to? Well, there are only so many colors a girl can dye her hair...
Okay, okay, I've finally got it. This idea is even better than the one about Santa Claus behind bars. We wire every card to give an electric shock when the envelope opens, and then we...
Thank goodness the man is harmless. Merry Christmas from the Carvins.
Just smile and keep quiet, Braden. If you get his attention, he'll draw you doing something really embarrassing...
Psst! Hey, Kate! Till death do us part and all that, but do I really have to be in your father's Christmas Cards?
1997

By 1998, with our eldest now married, we figured we'd made it – twenty-five years of marital bliss. (Mostly bliss, anyway.) Karen's endless patience was paying off.

 1998

1999 was full of predictions that catastrophe would strike when the world's computers could not recognize a new millennium. (It was all about extra zero digits.) We wondered if the Romans – whose numerals didn't include a zero – had similar fears.

1999

"THE ORIGINAL MILLENIUM BUG"
I'M SORRY, BUT OUR COMPUTERS DON'T SHOW ANYTHING AT ALL AFTER THE 24TH...
HEY BUD - WHAT YEAR WILL IT BE NEXT YEAR?
ZERO, I THINK...
HOW DO I WRITE THAT IN ROMAN NUMERALS?
COME TO THINK OF IT, WILL IT STILL BE 1 B.C. ON DECEMBER 26TH?
IV B.C.
III B.C.
WISHING YOU A HAPPY HOLIDAY AND A "GLITCH-FREE" NEW YEAR — THE CARVINS

 2000

人の間に平穏と友好を

Peace on Earth. Good Will Between Men.

From Karen, Joe, Jen, Daniel and Tessa Carvin,
and our exchange student, Rio Takeuchi.

12-7-00

2000

"Three Wise Men From the East"

In early times, the people of Japan spoke a beautiful language – but they had no system for writing it down. They couldn't make a list, write a poem, or send a love letter. Then, about the time of King Herod in the West, three wise men from the East (the Far East) came to Yamato bearing pictographs the Chinese used for writing.

The first wise man said to the people of Yamato: "Look. I will show you our word for "person." He drew a stick figure of a man walking: 人 The second wise man said, "Here is our word for the Sun." And he drew the Sun: 日 The third wise man said "We can even draw invisible things. If we draw a "gate" 門 with only the Sun 日 shining through 間, we mean the empty space between the gate posts, or any *space between* things.

A crowd gathered in the village, fascinated at the pictographs. "Show us more," they clamored. So the first wise man drew an infant in swaddling clothes, arms outstretched – the word for "child" 子. The second drew the child's mother, kneeling nearby – the word for "woman" 女, and said that by drawing the woman and child together 好 one could depict affection. The third wise man said that by adding two hands clasped together 友, one could depict friendship and good will. 友好

The people were excited by the pictographs. News of the wise men's gifts spread quickly. A hush fell over the crowd as the Emperor's daughter appeared and asked if the first wise man could draw a heart. He drew the main ventricle, with the three smaller compartments, and said "Yes, My lady, this is a heart: 心

The Emperor's daughter asked the second wise man, "How might I draw compassion?" And the second wise man answered her: "My lady, first draw a heart 心 then draw both a right hand 爫 and a left hand ヨ and place them over the heart. This is compassion 㥯.

Well pleased, the Emperor's daughter returned to the palace and told her father, the Emperor, about the pictographs. The Emperor summoned the three wise men to the palace. Addressing them, he asked: "Can you draw Peace throughout my Empire?"

The third wise man said to the Emperor: "Sire – to have Peace, you must begin with 㥯 compassion. But Peace also depends on prosperity. Add a rice plant 禾 to your drawing. Then you will have Peace 平穏

The next day, the Emperor's messengers delivered a piece of rice paper to every family in Yamato. On it was a message from the Emperor:

人の間に平穏と友好を

men between peace good will

Peace on Earth. Good Will Between Men.

2001 2001

A

Dictionary of Seasonal Greetings

Card 2001 Carvin

card, greeting (kärd, grē′ ting) *n.* **1.** A tradition started by Londoner William Maw Egley in 1842. **2.** In the 20th century, a multi-million dollar business for Hallmark. **3.** A personally crafted, individualized way we have of telling our friends what's going on in our lives, and wishing them well. [< Gk. *chartēs*, a leaf of paper + OE *grētan*, to hail, accost, or greet.]

carol (kar′-el) *n.* A song of joy or praise, especially one for a special event or holiday. [< Gk. *choros*, a dance.]

carve (kärv) *vb.* To cut or slice with a knife, as a holiday ham, turkey or goose. [< OE *ceorfan*, to cut.]

Carvin, Daniel (kär′-ven, dan′-yel) n. **1.** A 21 year old college student majoring in history at the University of South Florida. **2.** A voracious reader who also works at Publix and who, for sound budgetary reasons, still lives at home. **3.** A nightowl on line nightly from 10 p.m. until 5 a.m. at CptnBlammo@aol.com. **4.** A single man, the only son of Karen and Joseph Carvin. **5.** A six-foot tall household appliance, occasionally useful for mowing the lawn. [< Hebrew *Daniel*, meaning "God is my judge."]

Carvin, Jennifer (kär′-ven, jen′-i-fer) n. **1.** A 24 year old reformed accounting major, now pursuing a degree in elementary education at the University of South Florida. **2.** A single woman, second child of Karen and Joseph. **3.** A domestic chef two nights a week who specializes in healthful meals and chocolate chip cookies; a.k.a. *Jennyrelli.* **4.** A spelunker, skydiver and world traveler who, for sound budgetary reasons, still lives at home; reachable on-line at RinneyC@aol.com. [< Welsh *Jennifer*, "friend of peace."]

Carvin, Joseph (kär′-ven, jo′-zef) n. **1.** A 51 year old husband and father of four; a reformed lawyer now working at Publix; reachable at jwcarvin@aol.com. **2.** A recluse who emerges from his study, where he's currently writing a historical novel set in first century Macedonia, only to eat. **3.** An incurable word lover who will never own enough dictionaries or books on the origins of words. **4.** A designer of do-it-yourself greeting cards. [< Hebrew *Yoseph*, meaning "He will add."]

Carvin 2002 Christmas

Carvin, Karen (kär′-ven, kar′-en) n. **1.** A 48 year old domestic engineer and mother of four. **2.** A quilter, seamstress, and incurable dabbler in oils, acrylics, water colors and other decorative arts, reachable on-line at KLouC73@aol.com. **3.** A loyal wife who keeps her husband out of trouble by censoring his more outrageous ideas for seasonal greeting cards. **4.** A domestic chef (Saturday nights and holidays only!) [*Karen*, a Danish form of *Katherine* < Gk. *katharos*, clean and pure]

Carvin, Kathryn (kär′-ven, kath′-rin) n. **1.** Maiden name of Kathryn Way, a 27 year old elementary school teacher, wife of teacher Braden Way. (He threatens to send his children to her classroom when they're bad!) **2.** A member of the Virginia Boat Club, adept as both oarsman and coxswain, reachable on line at BKWAY1@mediaone.net. **3.** Eldest child of Karen and Joseph, now living "up north" in Richmond, who wisely lets her husband do the cooking. [< Gk. *katharos*, clean and pure]

Carvin, Tessa (kär′-ven, tes′-e) n. **1.** A 17 year old senior in the International Baccalaureate program at King High School in Tampa. **2.** An applicant to the University of Florida, reachable on-line at Maximuh02@aol.com. **4.** A domestic chef four nights a week, who'd have rather been a princess. **5.** Fourth child of Karen and Joseph. [< Gk. *tetra*, meaning four.]

celebrate (sel′-e-brāt) vb. To observe an event with joy [Latin *celeber*, famous.]

Chanukah (Khä′-noo-ke) n. **1.** Hannukah. **2.** A Jewish festival lasting eight days in memory of the rededication of the temple at Jerusalem. **3.** A time we wish our friends well, and send greeting cards. [< Hebrew *Honnukah*, dedication.]

chimney (chim′-nē) *n.* A chute over a fireplace, designed for smoke, not for large men in red suits. [< Gk. *kaminos*, an oven or kiln]

Christmas, Merry (krist′-mes, me′-rī) n. **1.** A Christian holiday in memory of the birth of Jesus of Nazareth. **2.** A day the chefs cook ham, turkey or goose, and Dad carves. **3.** What we wish our friends, right before wishing them a Happy New Year! [< Gk. *Christos*, meaning an anointed one.]

card, greeting (kärd, grē′ ting) *n.* **1.** A tradition started by Londoner William Maw Egley in 1842. **2.** In the 20th century, a multi-million dollar business for Hallmark. **3.** A personally crafted, individualized way we have of telling our friends what's going on in our lives, and wishing them well. [< Gk. *chartēs,* a leaf of paper + OE *grētan,* to hail, accost, or greet.]

carol (kar′-el) *n.* A song of joy or praise, especially one for a special event or holiday. [< Gk. *choros,* a dance.]

carve (kärv) *vb.* To cut or slice with a knife, as a holiday ham, turkey or goose. [< OE *ceorfan,* to cut.]

Carvin, Daniel (kär′-ven, dan′-yel) n. **1.** A 21 year old college student majoring in history at the University of South Florida. **2.** A voracious reader who also works at Publix and who, for sound budgetary reasons, still lives at home. **3.** A nightowl on line nightly from 10 p.m. until 5 a.m. at CptnBlammo@aol.com. **4.** A single man, the only son of Karen and Joseph Carvin. **5.** A six-foot tall household appliance, occasionally useful for mowing the lawn. [< Hebrew *Daniel,* meaning "God is my judge."]

Carvin, Jennifer (kär′-ven, jen′-i-fer) n. **1.** A 24 year old reformed accounting major, now pursuing a degree in elementary education at the University of South Florida. **2.** A single woman, second child of Karen and Joseph. **3.** A domestic chef two nights a week who specializes in healthful meals and chocolate chip cookies; a.k.a. *Jennyrelli.* **4.** A spelunker, skydiver and world traveler who, for sound budgetary reasons, still lives at home; reachable on-line at RinneyC@aol.com. [< Welsh *Jennifer,* "friend of peace."]

Carvin, Joseph (kär′-ven, jo′-zef) n. **1.** A 51 year old husband and father of four; a reformed lawyer now working at Publix; reachable at jwcarvin@aol.com. **2.** A recluse who emerges from his study, where he's currently writing a historical novel set in first century Macedonia, only to eat. **3.** An incurable word lover who will never own enough dictionaries or books on the origins of words. **4.** A designer of do-it-yourself greeting cards. [< Hebrew *Yoseph,* meaning "He will add."]

Carvin, Karen (kär′-ven, kar′-en) n. **1.** A 48 year old domestic engineer and mother of four. **2.** A quilter, seamstress, and incurable dabbler in oils, acrylics, water colors and other decorative arts, reachable on-line at KLouC73@aol.com. **3.** A loyal wife who keeps her husband out of trouble by censoring his more outrageous ideas for seasonal greeting cards. **4.** A domestic chef (Saturday nights and holidays only!) [*Karen,* a Danish form of *Katherine* < Gk. *katharos,* clean and pure]

Carvin, Kathryn (kär′-ven, kath′-rin) n. **1.** Maiden name of Kathryn Way, a 27 year old elementary school teacher, wife of teacher Braden Way. (He threatens to send his children to her classroom when they're bad!) **2.** A member of the Virginia Boat Club, adept as both oarsman and coxswain, reachable on line at BKWAY1@mediaone.net. **3.** Eldest child of Karen and Joseph, now living "up north" in Richmond, who wisely lets her husband do the cooking. [< Gk. *katharos,* clean and pure]

Carvin, Tessa (kär′-ven, tes′-e) n. **1.** A 17 year old senior in the International Baccalaureate program at King High School in Tampa. **2.** An applicant to the University of Florida, reachable on-line at Maximuh02@aol.com. **4.** A domestic chef four nights a week, who'd have rather been a princess. **5.** Fourth child of Karen and Joseph. [< Gk. *tetra,* meaning four.]

celebrate (sel′-e-brāt) vb. To observe an event with joy [Latin *celeber,* famous.]

Chanukah (Khä′-noo-ke) n. **1.** Hannukah. **2.** A Jewish festival lasting eight days in memory of the rededication of the temple at Jerusalem. **3.** A time we wish our friends well, and send greeting cards. [< Hebrew *Honnukah,* dedication.]

chimney (chim′-nē) *n.* A chute over a fireplace, designed for smoke, not for large men in red suits. [< Gk. *kaminos,* an oven or kiln]

Christmas, Merry (krist′-mes, me′-rī) n. **1.** A Christian holiday in memory of the birth of Jesus of Nazareth. **2.** A day the chefs cook ham, turkey or goose, and Dad carves. **3.** What we wish our friends, right before wishing them a Happy New Year! [< Gk. *Christos,* meaning an anointed one.]

With the kids finally grown, we looked forward to having an "empty nest."

Kate and Braden Way

Our eldest, Kate, married a fine young Man...

And Daniel, our son,
is soon off to Japan.

Tess is in Gainesville,
A Florida Gator...

And Jen's moving north to be an educator...

Bless the Season! Bless the day!
We're finally getting our own way!

After 30 years keeping them schooled and dressed, we're finally getting an Empty Nest!

But wait a minute, Karen – what did you say?
Some whimsical pun about "getting our own Way?"

Best wishes for the holiday season
and a blessed 2003

--Joe & Karen Carvin
(Gramps and Grandma)

Evan Way (due 2-5-03)

WHAT? QUIT WORK? ARE YOU CRAZY?
KAREN, YOU KNOW I'VE DONE MUCH CRAZIER THINGS...
LET'S SEE - LIKE THE TIME YOU TOOK A 2" BY 4" TO THE GAS GRILL?
EXACTLY! WE SURVIVED THAT, DIDN'T WE? I JUST NEED MORE TIME TO WRITE...
BUT JOE - WE'RE TALKING REAL LOSS OF INCOME HERE...
CAN'T YOU JUST THINK OF IT AS A CAREER CHANGE?
SURE I CAN. FROM "EMPLOYED" TO "UNEMPLOYED." GREAT CHANGE!
HOLD ON. I THINK I MAY BE GETTING SOME INSPIRATION HERE...
YOU KNOW, I DON'T KNOW IF I'M GOING TO BE ABLE TO STAND HIM BEING HOME EVERY DAY...
OKAY- I'VE GOT IT! HOW DOES THIS SOUND: "WHEN A MAN FALLS INTO HIS "ANECDOTAGE" IT'S A SIGN FOR HIM TO RETIRE FROM THIS WORLD." BENJAMIN DISRAELI SAID THAT. I LIKE IT!
LOOKS LIKE IT'S GOING TO BE A VERY INTERESTING YEAR AHEAD AT THE CARVINS. HOPE YOU HAVE A GREAT ONE YOURSELF!
FORGET RETIREMENT! I'M JUST ENTERING MY "ANECDOTAGE" A LITTLE EARLY!
HAPPY HOLIDAY!
12-1-03

Steeling herself to Joe, now a retiree, being home all the time, Karen sought refuge in being a grandmother.

Okay Joe, the theme is Christmas. The clue is "How Mary invited the wise men to stay for the night."
"A rest, ye very gentle men?"
I'm not sure that's right. How about this one: "*Not* an odd Byzantine?"
An "Evan Alexandrian"?
That fits! Now this: "A two year old in the kitchen."
"A Way in a Manger"?
Great! Now one more: "Every grandparents dream..."

SOU BET KIDSAREHERE
HAPPY HANNUKAH OVEN
MEEK REVERENT Y EVERL
A BE FEW YESSIR AT
CHRISTMAS WITH FAMILY
VA ARELETTERS ON MYLIST
I THINK
I'VE GOT IT!
AND GREETINGS FR
KAREN LIT FOR ALL
AHAPPY NEW YEAR 2006

Spending time with family really was our grand dream, but the "children" (and now *grand*children) were moving to Virginia. Our decision to leave Florida after so many years meant leaving behind a lot of memories. While the coffin may symbolize the interment of the past, it was actually a quandary whether to bring the haunted house prop with us.

Book titles: The Empty Nest, Florida State, USF, Univ of Florida, FSDA, Building with Barry, Bailey, The Color of Christmas, Hunter's Green, 9314 WPC, Building Furniture, Street Hockey, Publix, David's Fiftieth, Corinne's Fiftieth, Joe's 50th, Florida Life, Cage Stories, A Piece of the Pie, Kayaking, Softball, Poker Nite, Tuesdays with Karen, Stonebridge, Marking the Lawn for Boar, Bunko Nights, The Day Dad Came Out of the Den, How to Do Art, Christmas with Family, Carving House Nights, Evan & the Spider, Cooking with Joe, An Eye for Jalapenos, Food & Fun with P, E & J.

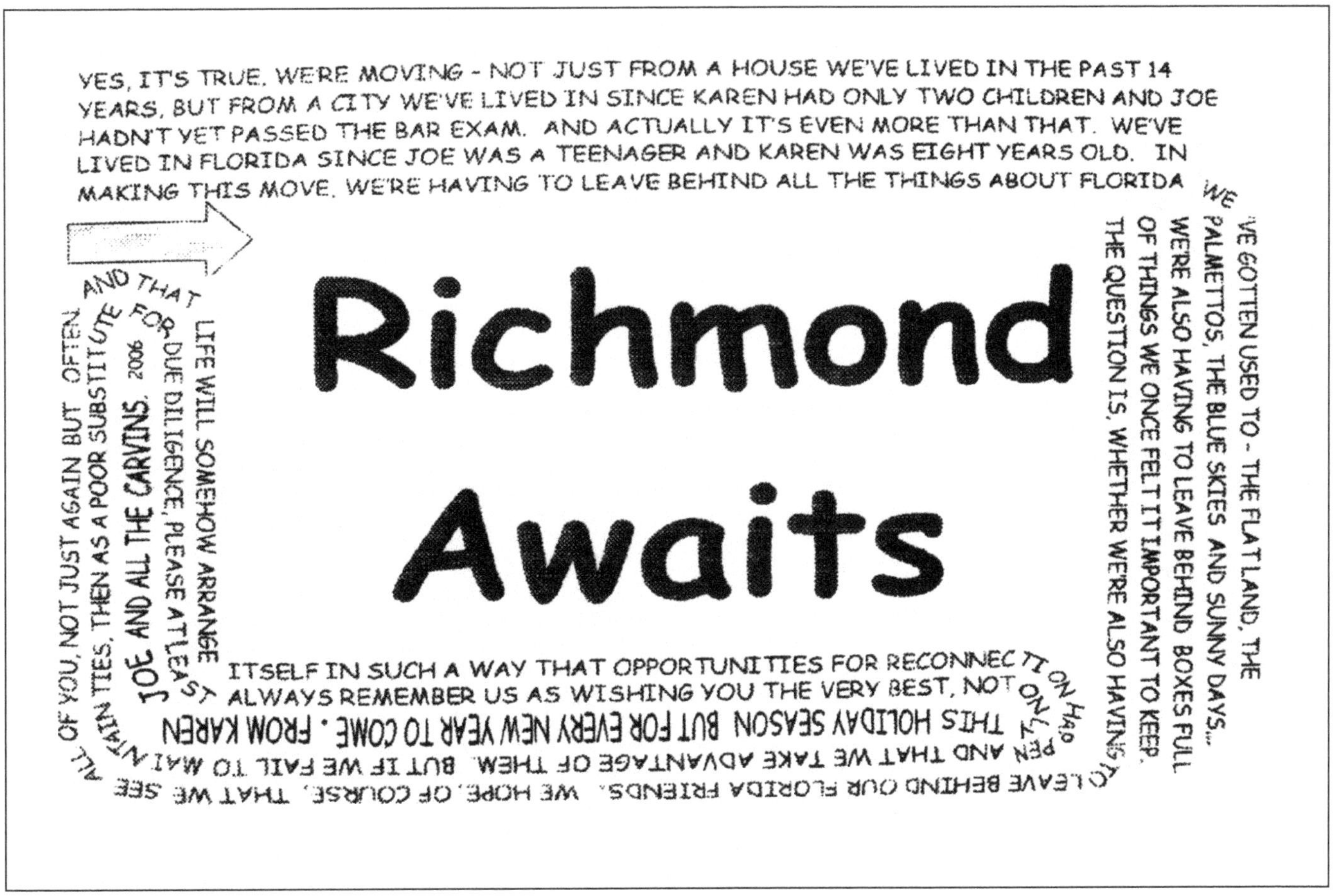
YES, IT'S TRUE. WE'RE MOVING - NOT JUST FROM A HOUSE WE'VE LIVED IN THE PAST 14 YEARS, BUT FROM A CITY WE'VE LIVED IN SINCE KAREN HAD ONLY TWO CHILDREN AND JOE HADN'T YET PASSED THE BAR EXAM. AND ACTUALLY IT'S EVEN MORE THAN THAT. WE'VE LIVED IN FLORIDA SINCE JOE WAS A TEENAGER AND KAREN WAS EIGHT YEARS OLD. IN MAKING THIS MOVE, WE'RE HAVING TO LEAVE BEHIND ALL THE THINGS ABOUT FLORIDA WE'VE GOTTEN USED TO - THE FLAT LAND, THE PALMETTOS, THE BLUE SKIES AND SUNNY DAYS... WE'RE ALSO HAVING TO LEAVE BEHIND BOXES FULL OF THINGS WE ONCE FELT IT IMPORTANT TO KEEP. THE QUESTION IS, WHETHER WE'RE ALSO HAVING TO LEAVE BEHIND OUR FLORIDA FRIENDS. WE HOPE, OF COURSE, THAT WE SEE ALL OF YOU, NOT JUST AGAIN BUT OFTEN AND THAT LIFE WILL SOMEHOW ARRANGE ITSELF IN SUCH A WAY THAT OPPORTUNITIES FOR RECONNECTION HAPPEN AND THAT WE TAKE ADVANTAGE OF THEM. BUT IF WE FAIL TO MAINTAIN TIES, THEN AS A POOR SUBSTITUTE FOR DUE DILIGENCE, PLEASE AT LEAST ALWAYS REMEMBER US AS WISHING YOU THE VERY BEST, NOT ONLY THIS HOLIDAY SEASON BUT FOR EVERY NEW YEAR TO COME. • FROM KAREN JOE AND ALL THE CARVINS. 2006
Richmond
Awaits

 2007

2007 was a difficult year. Daniel left the country to teach English in Japan, and the house in Tampa refused to sell. With two more grandchildren expected in May, Karen decided to go ahead and move to Virginia, to help with the newborns, leaving Joe behind in Tampa to pack, maintain, and sell the house. Nearly a year spent apart wasn't easy.

But the purchase of a house in Virginia, at year's end, helped inspire the year's card. It began small, a mere 3" by 3.5" in size, and unfolded.

This year brings
A new house
To call our own

[To find out how, unfold and read one step at a time.]

 2007

The spring arrivals of Jacob Nista and Rachel Way brought new cheer, and they also made their way into the card.

In April, we added
A grandson
Named Nista

[Now open here]

Jacob Matthew Nista
April 25, 2007

 2007

And in June
Our first,
Evan Way,
Got a sister

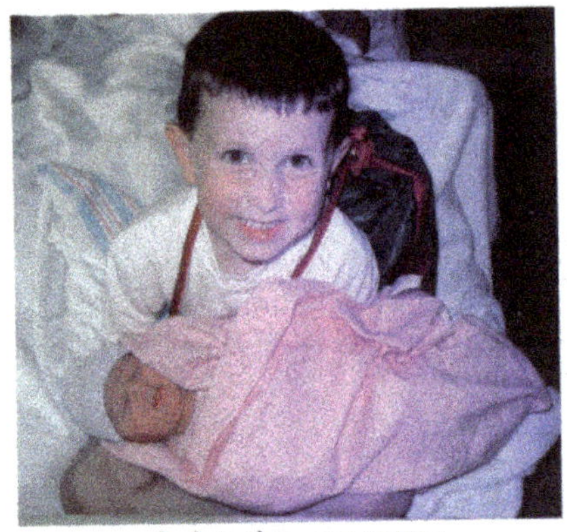

Rachel Delaney Way
June 1, 2007

Then, in Japan
On the tenth
Of November.....

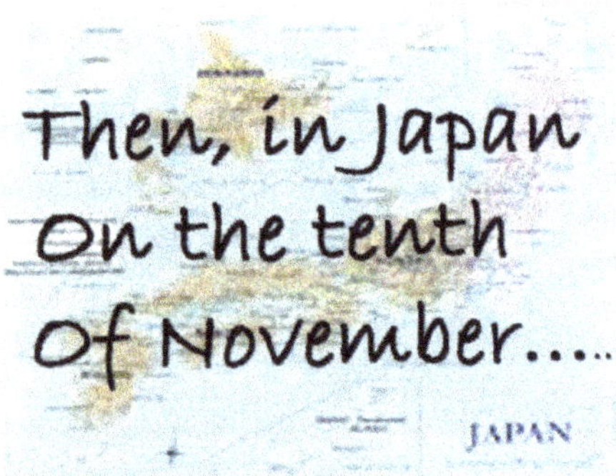

Pull down now

Thanks to Daniel and his new bride, Emiko, we attended a wonderful ("American style") wedding in Osaka, Japan, in which bride and groom arrived with fog and pyrotechnics, coming down stairs which descended from a two story ceiling.

And in June
Our first,
Evan Way,
Got a sister

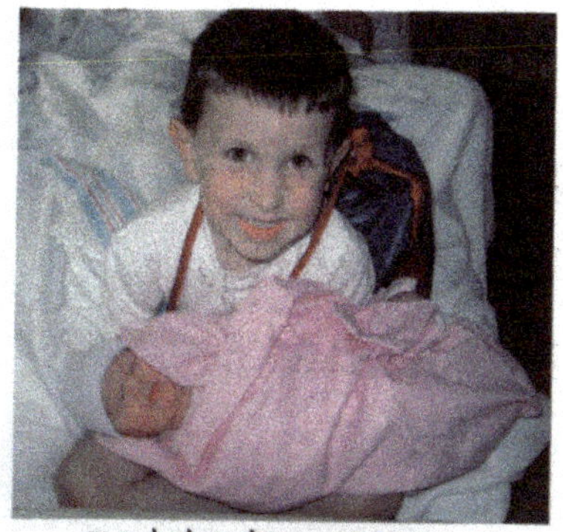

Rachel Delaney Way
June 1, 2007

Then, in Japan
On the tenth
Of November....

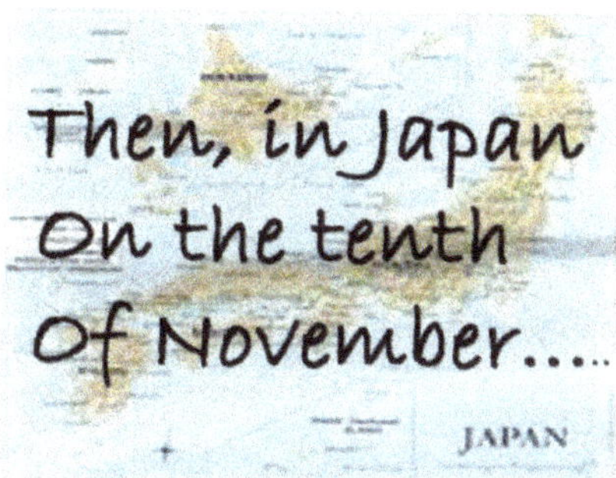

Our Daniel and Emi
Made an entrance
To remember...

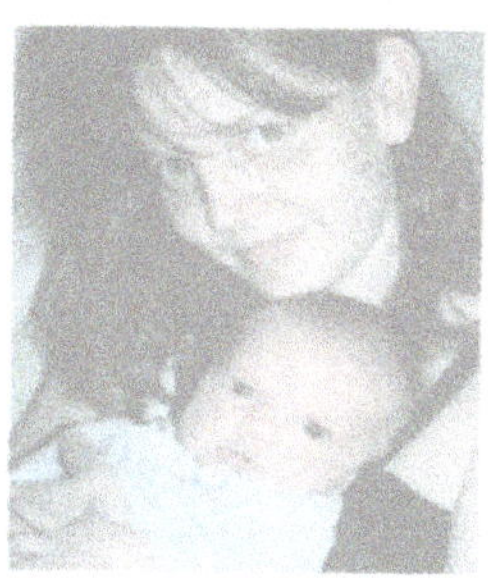

Jacob Matthew Nista
April 25, 2007

And Tessa, our youngest,
Wouldn't let us relax:
She added a little
Chihuahua named Max.

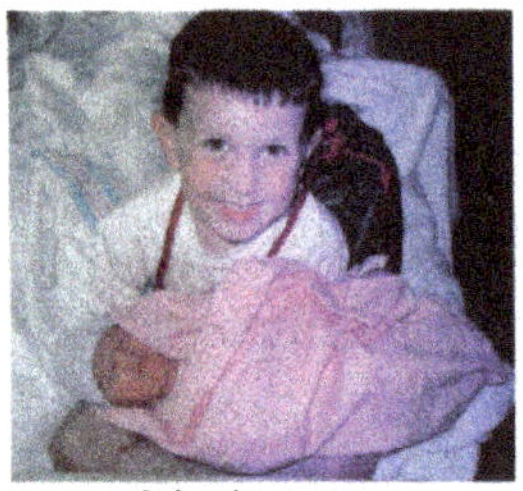

Rachel Delaney Way
June 1, 2007

And so you can see
How our family has grown:
We've got more than a house;
We've got plenty of home!
So when Wanderlust starts
To stir thoughts within ya,
Why not come and visit
Us here in Virginia?

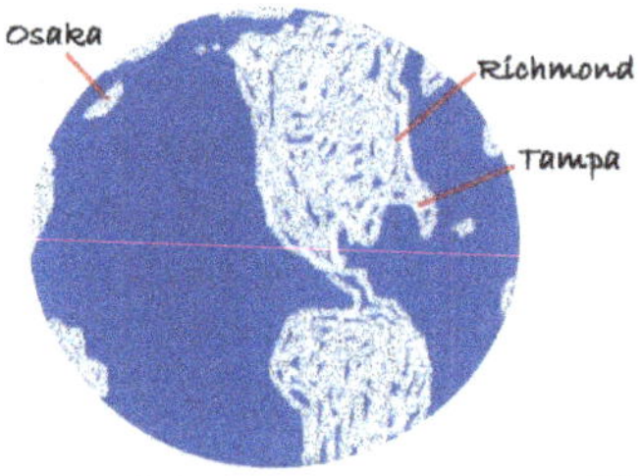

Our Daniel and Emi
Made an entrance
To remember...

May two thousand and eight
Bring you bright days, & snow,
And -- oh yes --
We nearly forgot --
An up-to-date picture
Of Karen and Joe...

Made in Japan
by Sudo Origami

2008

2008

This year....
The credit market dried up,
the housing market stalled,
and the stock market crashed
We can't sell our house in Tampa
and we're among Virginia's
unemployed.

But are we giving up? Hardly.
We have a plan for '09!
When you think about it,
all we need is food to eat and
the company of family and friends.
So why not come visit us
this holiday season?

P.S. Don't forget your spade and hoe.

-- Karen and Joe

 2009

SO - WHAT'S IT LIKE WITH a HOUSE FULL of GRANDKIDS EVERY DAY?
WELL, IN A WAY, IT'S LIKE EVERY DAY IS
GA GA GOO GOO

MERRY CHRISTMAS
At least, that's the way it feels at our house. We hope it's the same feeling at your place, every day and with every person you know
~ Karen & Joe Carvin 2009
Nonni
Evan
Rachel (Leo)
Poppi
Jacob
Jasper

Then Joe started to play golf. Doing so three times a week while Karen watched five infants in the house every day, Joe often forgot how good he had it.

REMEMBER HOW GOOD YOU HAVE IT
AND
HAVE A
HAPPY HOLIDAY
2010
Karen & Joe

Karen saw things a bit differently.

 2011

is being with family and friends

Not very original,
BUT VERY SINCERE.

Wishing you a 2012
filled with many blessings
Karen & Joe Carvin

 2011

What, me worry?

2012

So, people...
Years from now, what do you think we'll remember as the big events of 2012?
I got to ride on my Dad's Harley Davidson!
Are you serious? Rachel, what about the fact we started kindergarten? What about learning to read? What about the national debt crisis?
Oh come on, cousins... How about the arrival of another grandchild?
I think *I* know.
Yeah, Jasper, we know. The big news around here is that Paleo diet everybody's on...

HAPPY HOLIDAYS

Wishing you a sweet (but no added sugar or substitutes!)
and
healthy (no grains, no additives, no processed foods)

2013.

Eat only whole foods, like our ancestors did.

Hunt! Gather! Enjoy!

Karen and Joe Carvin
aka Nonni & Poppi

 2013

A
LOT
OF WORK
GOES INTO
40 YEARS
OF MARRIAGE
FOR THE PAST
39 OF THEM WE'VE
MADE OUR OWN
HOLIDAY CARDS
CHRONICLING OUR
GROWTH, FROM THE
EXCITEMENT OF AN-
TICIPATING OUR FIRST
DAUGHTER TO THE BIRTH
OF OUR 6TH GRANDCHILD.
THIS YEAR WE CELEBRATED 40
YEARS TOGETHER WITH TRIPS
TO THE BLUE RIDGE MOUNTAINS
& THE JOHN C. CAMPBELL FOLK SCHOOL
WHERE KAREN AND I HAVE TAKEN FELTING,
DYEING, SPLIT OAK BASKETRY, AND
BLOCK
CARVIN
G & PRI
NTING!

Happy holidays! Now that we've finished "making our own" and are enjoying retirement, Karen and I have entered a new phase of personal growth. We are enjoying the satisfaction of making our own things by hand, and appreciating the Folk School motto, "Sing behind the plow." The Folk School is about the joy of work by hand when it consists of making things in the company of others. Check out the Folk School at folkschool.org, and if blacksmithing, wood turning, pottery, spinning, weaving, dyeing, story-telling, banjo-playing or some other class sounds like your thing, let us know - we'd love to join you there for a week!
In the meantime, have a blessed and happy 2014... Karen & Joe Carvin

Front cover is a print from linoleum block by Joe. Scarves above dyed and made by Karen.

2014 2014

 2015

We made the folk school a recurring habit

If you believed in me.
Santa, I believe in you. But believe it or not, the sky, the land and the sea are paper too. The card itself is paper.
Are you sure all this paper isn't made of wood, like the rest of us?
Come to think of it, folks, we're all made of the same stuff
— The Carvings

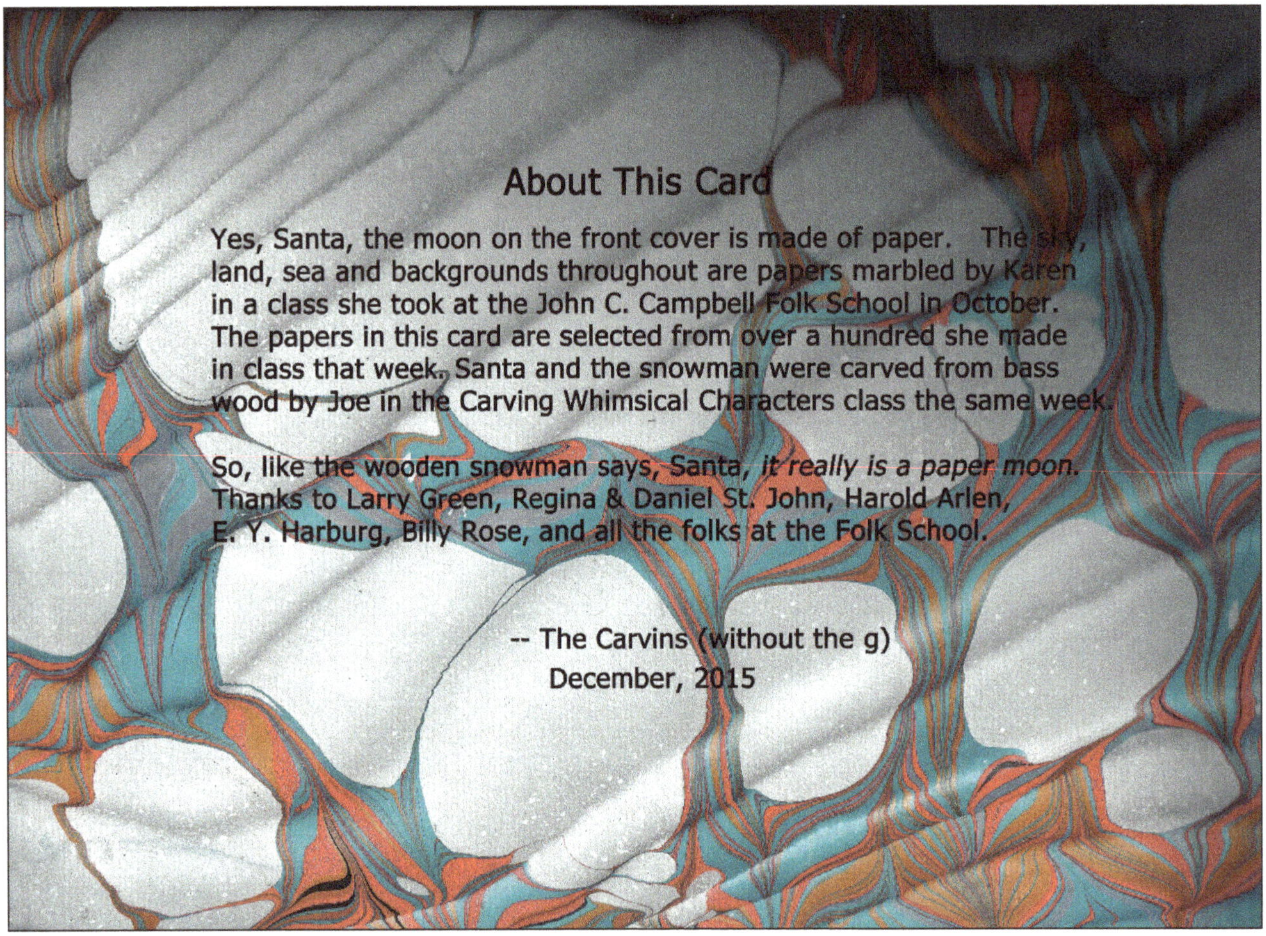

About This Card

Yes, Santa, the moon on the front cover is made of paper. The sky, land, sea and backgrounds throughout are papers marbled by Karen in a class she took at the John C. Campbell Folk School in October. The papers in this card are selected from over a hundred she made in class that week. Santa and the snowman were carved from bass wood by Joe in the Carving Whimsical Characters class the same week.

So, like the wooden snowman says, Santa, *it really is a paper moon.* Thanks to Larry Green, Regina & Daniel St. John, Harold Arlen, E. Y. Harburg, Billy Rose, and all the folks at the Folk School.

-- The Carvins (without the g)
December, 2015

In fact, we made so many things at the Folk School, we needed more pages in the year's holiday card to show it all off.

 2015

We carvings sure are fine and dandy pieces of work. How much we'd miss out on, if we were only two dimensions!
How boring life would be if we were all flat!
Right, Mrs. Mouse. Wood is taking over the Carving House by storm! We must be onto something special here.
Look, guys. You're okay, but you know what they say about 'dimentia.' Paper has its good sides, just like the rest of us.
I think time will tell...

How good can wood be, in a world of unlimited dimensions?

Then early this year, the Ways arrived –
With Kate, Evan & Rachel, the shoe slept five.
Five mouths to cook for; five beds to make;
Five sets of towels; five dinners to bake;
Five schedules to plan for; five bikes in the shed;
It was all they could do to keep themselves fed.

The next thing you know, Jen's family, the Nistas,
Moved in right next door, to be close to Jen's sister;
In the blink of an eye, Scott, Jake, Jasper, Jack, Jen
Turned the household of five into housing for ten!
Surrounded now by a burgeoning brood,
The woman did carpools, went shopping for food;
Taught art class on Wednesdays; ironed and sewed;
People wondered when she would overload.

But the woman kept out her welcome mat:
Of course there was room for Yoda, the cat.
And when the two dogs living next door at Jen's
Were joined by a baker's dozen of hens,
The woman just rubbed her sore back and legs
And thanked the good Lord that chickens lay eggs.

Then came the theater, and curious crowds;
The grandchildren danced, and sang songs, and bowed.
Guests by the dozens appeared in the yard –
(Too many, by far, to fit into the card.)

So…

HAPPY HOLIDAYS
and Best Wishes for 2018
from Karen & Joe

Dear Cousins: So. You think, just because I don't live in Virginia, you can be in Nonni and Poppi's Christmas card without me? Hah! What do you think of THESE poses?
-- Ryu

By 2018, we were contemplating the wider family.

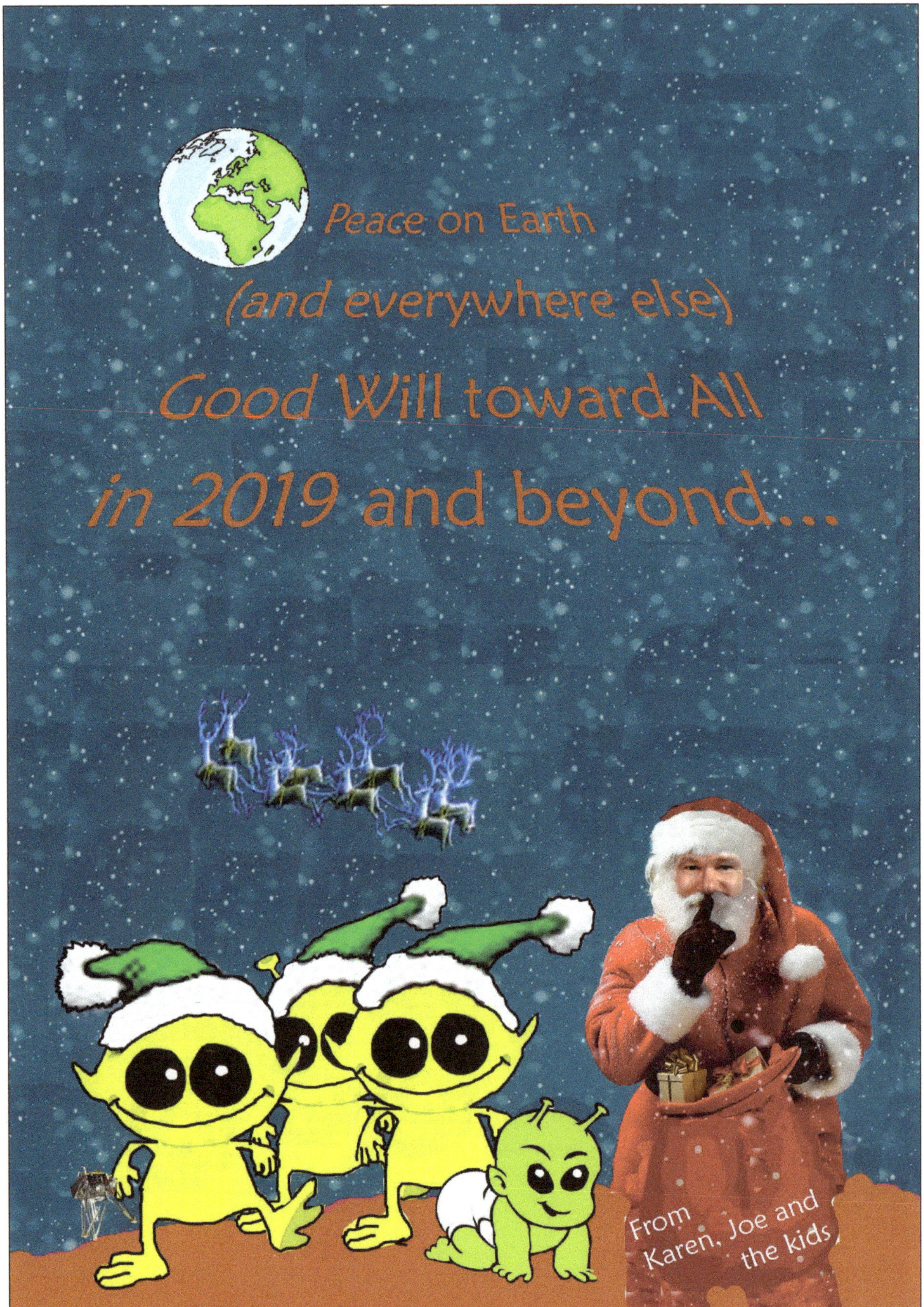
Peace on Earth
(and everywhere else)
Good Will toward All
in 2019 and beyond...
From
Karen, Joe and
the kids

 2018

Dear Friends,

It seems to us that we of Planet Earth are going to need to work together if there's to be anything left for our grandchildren. And that in doing so, we need to think less of our rights and more of our responsibilities, especially to those who are neither from blue states nor red, from East nor West, but still awaiting their time in this place we're lucky to call home.

May you enjoy a peaceful and productive new year

Karen & Joe.

jwcarvin.com

wemaybewrong.org

Joe, do you realize
what this means?

 2019

Nothing in Common

The bird's eye view:
Seems like every passing year we feel
A little more endangered. But our health is good.
Joe is working on several books,
Karen is quilting like crazy,
And the chickens are happy.
(Oh, yeah, the kids and grandkids are happy, too.)
What more can a couple of old coots expect?
Hope all is well with you and yours.

 2020

Merry Christmas
from our house(s)
to yours
2 daughters, 1 son-in-law,
3 grandchildren,
5 dogs, 1 gecko,
1 bird, 1 hamster
1 bearded dragon
11 chickens
1 daughter
2 teenagers
1 bearded dragon
1 dog, 1 cat,
and the two of us
12 ft
The Carvins

BE KIND
Everyone is fighting a hard battle.

Wishing you a thoughtful, loving 2022.
- Karen & Joe Carvin
We don't know what we don't know...

 2022

Two years ago, when Joe wrote a book about the story of life on earth, such life was four billion years old. By that reckoning, it's now been 4,000,000,002 years.

Meanwhile, Joe has now turned 72 and Karen 69. There are times we feel old, but the four-billion-year picture makes us feel very, very young!

Because she's taken up knitting and has lots of grandchildren to chauffeur, it looks like Karen may fall short of her goal to make four billion quilts in her lifetime, but she's working on it, and remains determined.

Joe, meanwhile, continues to write, and is still trying to express a coherent thought in fewer than four billion words.

Anyway, with all these numbers in mind, we wanted to wish you happy holidays. So here's wishing you *four billion and three* moments of joy in 2023. (That's about 126 moments of joy every second!)

Youthfully yours,
Karen & Joe Carvin

Which brings us to *this* year...

2023 2023

We wish you happy holidays and all the best things for the years yet to come!

Karen Joe

Don't forget, Joe... Back on page 1996, we promised answers...

CARVIN FAMILY TRIVIA QUIZ	ANSWERS	
a. Our Scottish Greatgrandfather gave his small Texas Ranch this name	a. W E E	115 5 140
b. Chore the young man of the house does faithfully	b. E M P T Y T H E T R A S H	142 41 72 46 35 153 145 12 49 146 68 40 194
c. Jennifer works hard to maximize her minimum ______.	c. W A G E S	54 176 187 139 135
d. A liqueur named for the Carvin family dog (or for Mrs. O'Leary's cow?)	d. I R I S H C R E A M	77 4 16 148 80 144 14 175 59 11
e. What Dad's monkey did from the tree limbs in '62	e. S W U N G	78 157 183 17 91
f. The household projects Dad still hasn't gotten to?	f. H O N E Y D U E S	116 161 74 119 167 58 37 61 164
g. Wind-up string toy from Mom's youth	g. Y O Y O	43 169 15 2
h. North Carolina River where Dad's kayak longs to play	h. O C O E E	123 20 29 21 102
i. What the family that prays together achieves	i. U N I T Y	132 156 120 141 98
j. What "X" (see below) strives to be at the courts	j. A T E N N I S A C E	155 179 134 18 122 32 87 89 110 95
k. Kate and Braden's big day	k. M A Y T H I R D	101 62 90 70 178 117 13 88
l. One of Dad's many uses for that ol' demon rum....	l. E G G N O G	26 34 63 190 99 1
m. "_____ ____ virgin mother & child..."	m. R O U N D Y O N	103 186 162 22 38 8 160 57
n. Second of the notes Dad croons at karaoke	n. R E	133 172
o. Word that goes well with "truly" and "sincerely"	o. Y O U R S	168 109 100 104 185
p. Jennifer's middle name	p. C O R I N N E	127 9 143 51 107 191 189
q. Where we play golf and tennis	q. H U N T E R S G R E E N C O U N T R Y C L U B	154 56 60 23 158 163 96 53 81 64 111 47 124 48 174 33 177 69 181 79 25 170 171
r. Though over 9 pounds, Jen was still the ____ of the litter. ("X" was 12 lbs. 7 oz.)	r. R U N T	94 10 126 75
s. What Mom is, when not painting	s. I N T O Q U I L T S	82 130 30 73 173 71 39 44 149 83
t. What Uncle Chris may do if you don't play your cards right	t. S H O O T T H E M O O N	152 66 182 19 27 7 50 67 85 55 180 108
u. Now 12, she was named "4th" (in Greek)	u. T E S S A	159 45 6 137 86
v. Chore the young man of the house hates to do	v. M O W T H E Y A R D	165 92 138 97 76 129 105 166 184 131
w. What Mom uses for that special, "crafty" touch	w. A R T I S T S H A N D	136 65 84 147 193 113 24 31 42 112 188
x. What Mom and Dad have (& Johnny Cash doesn't?)	x. S O N N A M E D D A N I E L	114 36 121 28 192 150 125 93 3 151 52 106 128 118

Puzzle Square - & Bonus Message

■	G 1L	O 2g	D 3x	■	R 4d	E 5a	S 6u	T 7t	■	Y 8m	O 9p	U 10r	■	M 11d	E 12b	R 13k
R 14d	Y 15g	■	I 16d	N 17e	N 18j	O 19t	C 20h	E 21h	N 22m	T 23q	S 24w	■	L 25q	E 26L	T 27t	■
N 28x	O 29h	T 30s	H 31w	I 32j	N 33q	G 34L	■	Y 35b	O 36x	U 37f	■	D 38m	I 39s	S 40b	M 41b	A 42w
Y 43g	■	L 44s	E 45u	T 46b	■	N 47q	O 48q	T 49b	H 50t	I 51p	N 52x	G 53q	■	W 54c	O 55t	U 56q
N 57m	D 58f	■	A 59d	N 60q	■	E 61f	A 62k	G 63L	E 64q	R 65w	■	H 66t	E 67t	A 68b	R 69q	T 70k
■	U 71s	P 72b	O 73s	N 74f	■	T 75r	H 76v	I 77d	S 78e	■	C 79q	H 80d	R 81q	I 82s	S 83s	T 84w
M 85t	A 86u	S 87j	■	D 88k	A 89j	Y 90k	■	G 91e	O 92v	D 93x	■	R 94r	E 95j	S 96q	T 97v	■
Y 98i	O 99L	U 100o	■	M 101k	E 102h	R 103m	R 104o	Y 105v	■	I 106x	N 107p	N 108t	O 109o	C 110j	E 111q	N 112w
T 113w	S 114x	■	W 115a	H 116f	I 117k	L 118x	E 119f	■	I 120i	N 121x	N 122j	O 123h	C 124q	E 125x	N 126r	C 127p
E 128x	■	E 129v	N 130s	D 131v	U 132i	R 133n	E 134j	S 135c	■	A 136w	■	S 137u	W 138v	E 139c	E 140a	T 141i
E 142b	R 143p	■	C 144d	H 145b	R 146b	I 147w	S 148d	T 149s	M 150x	A 151x	S 152t	■	T 153b	H 154q	A 155j	N 156i
■	W 157e	E 158q	■	T 159u	O 160m	■	O 161f	U 162m	R 163q	S 164f	■	M 165v	A 166v	Y 167f	■	Y 168o
O 169g	U 170q	■	B 171q	E 172n	Q 173s	U 174q	E 175d	A 176c	T 177q	H 178k	■	T 179j	O 180t	■	Y 181q	O 182t
U 183e	R 184v	S 185o	■	■	■	O 186m	G 187c	D 188w	E 189p	N 190L	■	N 191p	A 192x	S 193w	H 194b	■

www.ingramcontent.com/pod-product-compliance
Ingram Content Group UK Ltd.
Pitfield, Milton Keynes, MK11 3LW, UK
UKHW060125010826
14089UKWH00006B/163

9 798986 186818